LEADERSHIP SKILLS FOR WOMEN

Revised Edition

Marilyn Manning, Ph. D.,
with Patricia Haddock

A FIFTY-MINUTE™ SERIES BOOK

CRISP PUBLICATIONS, INC.
Menlo Park, California

LEADERSHIP SKILLS FOR WOMEN
Revised Edition
Marilyn Manning, Ph. D., with Patricia Haddock

CREDITS
Editor: **Michael G. Crisp**
Typesetting: **Interface Studio**
Cover Design: **Carol Harris**
Artwork: **Ralph Mapson**

Copyright © 1989, 1995 by Crisp Publications, Inc.
Printed in the United States of America

Distribution to the U.S. Trade:

National Book Network, Inc.
4720 Boston Way
Lanham, MD 20706
1-800-462-6420

Distribution to the Canadian Trade:

Raincoast Books
8680 Cambie Street
Vancouver, B.C.
V6P 6M9
604-323-7100
800-663-5714

Library of Congress Catalog Card Number 94-80009
Manning, Marilyn and Haddock, Patricia
Leadership Skills for Women
ISBN 1-56052-325-5

This book is printed on recyclable paper with soy ink.

TO THE READER

You have worked long and hard to reach your present position. In the process, you have observed successful leaders in action. Chances are, you have formed opinions of what makes leaders effective or ineffective.

People don't develop leadership skills by waving a magic wand or reciting the perfect word. No one becomes a good leader overnight.

The seeds of good leadership come from a combination of personal skills, talent, and character. You shape and nurture your leadership style by strengthening your talents, working to eliminate problem behaviors, and learning to develop new, more productive ones.

So, why in this book, have we concentrated on female leaders?

Everything you have learned, absorbed, and observed over your lifetime has influenced your behavior. This means that gender and gender-specific behaviors play a part in your leadership style. This book will show you how to use your unique talents, *plus* your feminine strengths, to become the best leader possible, both on the job and in your personal life.

Good luck!

Marilyn Manning   and   Patricia Haddock

ABOUT THIS BOOK

LEADERSHIP SKILLS FOR WOMEN is not like most books. It has a unique ''self-paced'' format that encourages a reader to become personally involved. Designed to be ''read with a pencil,'' there are an abundance of exercises, activities, assessments and cases that invite participation.

The objective of LEADERSHIP SKILLS FOR WOMEN is to provide information that will help a reader understand the qualities that make people leaders, and then teach basic leadership skills that can be applied in the work place. The emphasis is on women and the book addresses unique challenges and opportunities women leaders face.

LEADERSHIP SKILLS FOR WOMEN (and other self-improvement titles listed in the back of this book) can be used effectively in a number of ways. Here are some possibilities:

—Individual Study. Because the book is self-instructional, all that is needed is a quiet place, some time and a pencil. By completing the activities and exercises, a reader should not only receive valuable feedback, but also practical steps for self-improvement.

—Workshops and Seminars. The book is ideal for assigned reading prior to a workshop or seminar. With the basics in hand, the quality of the participation will improve, and more time can be spent on concept extensions and applications during the program. The book is also effective when it is distributed at the beginning of a session, and participants ''work through'' the contents.

—Remote Location Training. Books can be sent to those not able to attend ''home office'' training sessions.

There are other possibilities that depend on the objectives, program, or ideas of the user. One thing for sure, even after it has been read, this book will be looked at—and thought about—again and again.

TABLE OF CONTENTS

SECTION I

THE CHARACTERISTICS OF EFFECTIVE LEADERS

> "I have very strong feelings about how you lead your life. You always look ahead, you never look back."
>
> *Ann Richards*
> Politician

CHARACTERISTICS OF EFFECTIVE LEADERS

"Manager" and "supervisor" are labels that are often used interchangeably in job descriptions. You may carry either title, but neither automatically makes you a leader.

The title of "leader" must be earned by inspiring and motivating people to give their best. A successful leader commits herself to her organization and fosters that same kind of commitment in her followers.

The successful leader:
- Knows her job and her field thoroughly.
- Stays on top of current developments, trends, and theories.
- Knows her people, including their strengths, weaknesses, hopes, and goals.
- Shares a vision of service, excellence, ethics, and achievement with others.
- Demonstrates by her words and actions strength of character and integrity.

Characteristics of:	
Good listener	Good communicator
Accessible	Says "no"
Decisive	Avoids quick judgements
Gracious	Acknowledges strengths
Keeps it simple	Untangles complications
Optimistic outlook	Realistic
Gives credit	Takes credit when appropriate
Solves problems	Avoids office politics
Speaks directly	Understand how systems work
Acknowledges mistakes	Requires accountability
Says "Yes"	Explains why
Enthusiastic	Calm
Values intuition	Is inflexible
Likes challenges	Values diversity
Ethical	Visionary

TEST YOUR LEADERSHIP POTENTIAL

	Usually	Sometimes	Rarely
1. I look for positive challenges during periods of change.	_____	_____	_____
2. I am decisive, willing to take risks, and learn from mistakes.	_____	_____	_____
3. I regularly acknowledge others' accomplishments.	_____	_____	_____
4. I reflect the values I believe.	_____	_____	_____
5. I look for ways to share power.	_____	_____	_____
6. I delegate tasks with authority and decisiveness.	_____	_____	_____
7. I have written long range plans and I am committed to them.	_____	_____	_____
8. I create a motivational environment.	_____	_____	_____
9. I promote team effort and spirit.	_____	_____	_____
10. I regularly give honest, constructive feedback to my team.	_____	_____	_____
11. I make decisions in a timely manner.	_____	_____	_____
12. I stand up for what I believe.	_____	_____	_____
13. I expect to be treated with respect at all times.	_____	_____	_____
14. I respect the people who work for me.	_____	_____	_____
15. I clearly state my expectations.	_____	_____	_____
16. I evaluate what others have to say, but take full responsibility for the decisions I make.	_____	_____	_____

Striving to answer "Yes" on each of these questions is a worthy goal for any leader especially for women leaders who sometimes feel that they must compromise more than male leaders. Any questions you answered with "Sometimes" or "No", should become your goals as you study this book.

List your leadership goals below: For instance, "I will look for opportunities to be more decisive."

Goal 1.

Goal 2.

Goal 3.

Goal 4.

Goal 5.

MANY "STYLES" OF LEADERSHIP

There are as many leadership "styles" as there are leaders. Many will work, but some are more effective than others.

Generally, an effective leadership style will allow you to:
- identify and target realistic and relevant goals;
- produce realistic and relevant results;
- align your goals to stated business objectives;
- design performance requirements that are based on measurable items such as, quality, quantity, cost, timeliness, and profit;
- revise plans as necessary;
- keep lines of communication open.
- maintain your integrity and ethical standards.

To the extent any management style hinders you, it is ineffective and should be changed.

For a good book on how to align employee performance with goals, order *Effective Performance Appraisals* by Robert B. Maddux. See the back of this book for ordering information.

WHAT STYLE ARE YOU?

As you read through the following characteristics of leadership styles, circle with a <u>blue</u> pen those attributes that describe you. Then, go over the items you circled in blue and mark with a <u>yellow</u> highlighter any characteristics you believe may be detrimental to your effectiveness. Finally, read the lists again and circle with a <u>red</u> pen attributes you think would be beneficial for you to develop.

After you finish this exercise, you should have a clear picture of your current leadership assets and liabilities. Using what you have recorded, you can put together a plan to become a more effective leader.

You may find it helpful to observe the workstyles of your employees and adjust your style accordingly. This is called "situational leadership" and it can be very powerful. For example, when you approach an "analytical" employee, you should prepare details and communicate in a highly methodical way. If your style is naturally different, (for instance if you are a "charismatic,") your enthusiasm and need to persuade might make you ineffective leading an "analyzer." You will have many opportunities to recognize and practice situational leadership throughout this book.

There are two primary leadership styles: either quiet or outgoing. Many women often relate more strongly to the quiet styles, often because of their upbringing and societal expectations. While most people will find one style more dominant, you can strengthen your leadership skills by cultivating characteristics of the less dominant style. This can give you more behavioral options and responses, and make you more effective.

STYLE #1: *Quiet Styles*	
Traditional team player:	**Analytical problem solver:**
The Supporter	**The Perfectionist**
Major flaw: Agrees too much	Major flaw: Questions too much
Likeable Helpful Easy-going Patient Deliberate Calm Low-risk taker Loyal Predictable Team player	Conscientious Reserved Fretful Mature Perfectionist Systematic Accurate High standards Self-disiplined Orderly

STYLE #2: *Outgoing Styles*	
Dominant, controlling:	**Charismatic motivator:**
The Director	**The Motivator**
Major flaw: Directs too much	Major flaw: Talks too much
Direct Risk-taking Organizer Energizing Self-confident Fast-thinking Responsible Forceful Powerful Ambitious	Enthusiastic Influential Sympathetic Generous Gregarious Friendly Social Dramatic Loves recognition Charismatic

A LEADER'S ATTITUDE AFFECTS PRODUCTIVITY

Your attitude as a leader will set the pace and tone for your employees. People tend to mirror each other, and employees especially tend to mirror their managers.

If your attitude is positive and dynamic, people you work with will reflect your attitude by becoming more positive and dynamic. If, however, you complain and play the victim, you will find yourself surrounded by reflections of yourself.

Your attitude also will affect your team's productivity. When you develop good relationships with your employees and consistently project a positive attitude, they will tend to respond to that by being more productive.

But no one can be upbeat all the time. Sometimes personal problems, health problems, and people problems seem to conspire to erode our positive feelings and attitude.

Following are some tips to help you keep your attitude positive, especially during those ''down'' times:*

- Engage in a regular exercise program.

- Inject humor into your life and your workplace.

- Break major goals into smaller, more easily attainable ones.

- Take frequent, short, time-outs during the day for renewal.

- Balance work and leisure more effectively.

- Try volunteering to add perspective and depth to your life.

- Keep yourself looking professional.

- Find someone you trust as a role model, confidante, and sounding board.

- Ask for help when you need it and when it is appropriate.

- Spend time on a favorite activity or with a favorite person.

(*Adapted from *Attitude: Your Most Priceless Possession* by Elwood N. Chapman. See the back of this book for ordering information.)

A LEADER'S ATTITUDE AFFECTS PRODUCTIVITY (Continued)

LEADERSHIP EXERCISE

Rate your current attitude. Read each statement and circle the number you feel represents where you belong on the attitude scale. If you circle a 10, you are saying your attitude can not be improved in this area; if you circle a 1, you are saying your attitude could not be worse. Be honest.

	HIGH (Positive)					LOW (Negative)				
1. My feeling is that my boss would currently rate my attitude as:	10	9	8	7	6	5	4	3	2	1
2. Given the same choice, my co-workers would rate my attitude as:	10	9	8	7	6	5	4	3	2	1
3. Given the same choice, my family would rate my attitude as:	10	9	8	7	6	5	4	3	2	1
4. Given the same choice, my employees would rate my attitude as:	10	9	8	7	6	5	4	3	2	1
5. Realistically, I would rate my attitude as:	10	9	8	7	6	5	4	3	2	1
6. My effectiveness level is:	10	9	8	7	6	5	4	3	2	1
7. My creativity level is:	10	9	8	7	6	5	4	3	2	1
8. My enthusiasm toward my job is:	10	9	8	7	6	5	4	3	2	1
9. My enthusiasm toward my life is:	10	9	8	7	6	5	4	3	2	1
10. My recent disposition—the patience and sensitivity I show to others—deserves a rating of:	10	9	8	7	6	5	4	3	2	1

Your TOTAL score: _____

A score of 90 or more is a signal that your attitude is "in tune" and no adjustments seem necessary; a score between 70 and 89 indicates that minor adjustments may help; a rating between 50 and 69 suggests a major adjustment; if you rated yourself below 50, a complete overhaul may be required. Take some time to identify what is contributing to your negative attitude and to determine how you can change or eliminate the causes.

(Adapted from *Professional Excellence for Secretaries* by Marilyn Manning and Carolyn Barnes. See the back of this book for ordering information.)

A LEADER'S ATTITUDE AND VISION

> "Any of us can dream, but seeking vision is always done not only to heal and fulfill one's own potential, but also to learn to use that potential to serve all our relations: the two-leggeds, the four-leggeds, the wingeds, those that crawl upon the Earth, and the Mother Earth herself."
>
> *Brooke Medicine Eagle*
> Poet

Regardless of style, all business leaders take the role of manager and add a "plus" factor to it. That "plus" factor is called vision.

YOUR VISION

Your vision should:
• dovetail and support your organization's goals and/or mission statement, and
• reflect your ethics and commitment to the organization you work for.

You communicate vision by stating it simply and understandably. Write it down. Publish it for others to see. Tie it into job descriptions, assignments, performance plans, and work, individual and departmental goals. Never let your people forget the common vision they share.

A leader with vision is a person who:

• adheres to ethical standards.

• inspires and motivates.

• projects into the future and communicates a global outlook.

• obtains significant, often extraordinary, results from people.

• is highly committed to excellence, honesty, and productivity.

• expects and requires the commitment of others.

• is an effective listener.

YOUR VISION (Continued)

Take a few minutes to think about your work-related vision and then summarize it in the space provided below. You will have an opportunity to review and revise what you have written at the end of this book. Make sure your vision supports the goals and mission of your organization. After you have clearly described your vision, put it in writing and review it daily and communicate it to your employees.

When you define your vision, think about how it fits in with your vision for the other areas of your life. You want to ensure that you have congruity among all areas of your life—both work and personal. If you discover incongruities, take time to resolve them. Unresolved conflicts between your work and your personal life can lead to stress and poor performance. They weaken your effectiveness as a leader.

MY VISION IS: _____

_____

_____

_____

_____

_____

_____

_____

_____

_____

_____

_____

_____

_____

_____

_____

_____

_____

YOUR VISION (Continued)

Defining your values helps you support your vision.

On a piece of paper, draw a vertical line down the middle. On one side, list the values you wish to promote on the job.

Now, think back to your action during the past month (refer to your calendar and memos to assist you in recalling actions you took). Then, in the other column, write actions you took that demonstrated your commitment to your values. Take a moment to compare these values with your personal values and actions outside the job. Is there congruity or conflict?

EXAMPLE:

Values I promote on the job:	Actions I take:
Open, honest communication	I completed a written performance evaluation for Jack Roberts on March 15th and reviewed it with him in a face-to-face meeting. (Note: I do this for each of my employees every six months.)

ADD YOUR OWN:

Values I promote on the job:	Actions I take:

IDENTIFYING A LEADERSHIP MODEL

Think about and respond in writing to the following statements and questions:

1. I consider _____ to be a good leader.

(NAME)

2. The following qualities make this person a good leader: _____ .

   _____

3. I display the following similar qualities to _____ .

(NAME)

4. I do not display the following similar qualities to _____ .

(NAME)

5. I consider my greatest, most unique talents to be: _____ .

   _____

6. What can I learn about effective leadership by studying the leadership style of

   _____ identified in statement 1?

(NAME)

7. How can I go about studying this person's leadership style?_____ .

   _____

8. What characteristics of this person's style can I adopt right now?_____ .

   _____

9. How would I behave differently if I adopt these characteristics?_____ .

   _____

LEADERSHIP FUNCTIONS

Men and women may differ in styles, approaches, or attributes. Regardless, mastering the basic functions of leadership—planning, organizing, staffing and controlling—are essential to men and women becoming effective leaders.

QUICK CHECK

Place a "+" beside each of the following functions that are your strongest. Place a "✓" beside those that need the most development.

_____ **Plan.** Decide who, what, when, where, why and how things will be done, in view of the organization's goals and, if applicable, the team's capabilities; develop and interpret policies; manage budgets and continuously improve methods of performing specific tasks.

_____ **Organize.** Prepare schedules, delegate tasks and monitor progress through timetables or measurable objectives.

_____ **Staff.** Advise and support associates, recommend qualified team members for hire and promotion; evaluate individual and group performance; develop and reward associates.

_____ **Direct.** Motivate, inspire, and communicate with associates for better understanding, ownership and commitment; seek to reduce response or process time by encouraging innovation.

_____ **Control.** Measure performance, establish standards and measurements of quality and service, prevent and correct problems that impede effectiveness, and obtain feedback for current and future projects.

What particular tasks or projects can help you develop these abilities? To expedite the process, consider setting relevant goals to help you develop one or more of these areas.

Adapted from *The Woman Manager* by Connie Sitterly. See the back of this book for ordering information.

PREJUDICES AGAINST WOMEN
AS LEADERS

Despite significant inroads made by the feminist and civil rights movements, women still face unspoken prejudices and even harassment in the workplace. Sometimes these problems come to the foreground when a woman assumes a leadership role. You must be aware of them in order to protect yourself.

I have experienced or witnessed the belief stated by others that:

STEREOTYPES

- [ ] Women fall apart when the going gets rough.

- [ ] Women are catty or love to gossip.

- [ ] Women are afraid to make decisions or always change their minds.

- [ ] Women are too picky.

- [ ] Women use sex to get what they want.

- [ ] Women can be pushy and mouthy.

- [ ] Women are difficult to work for.

- [ ] Women aren't able to see the big picture.

- [ ] Women take things too personally.

- [ ] Women aren't good team players.

- [ ] Women are too soft to make decisions.

- [ ] Women allow their families or personal lives to get in the way of the job.

- [ ] Women no sooner get trained than they leave to have a baby.

(Continued next page)

STEREOTYPES (Continued)

☐ Women are too emotional and cry too easily.

☐ Women can't travel on business because of personal and family commitments.

☐ Women make things more complicated than they really are.

☐ Women are moody, especially at "that" time of the month.

☐ Women are inconsistent and fickle and don't know what they want.

☐ Women must agree to sex to get ahead.

List any of your behaviors that might relate to these beliefs and develop action steps to change your behavior.

Example: Stereotype: I can't make up my mind.
              Resolution: I will act more decisively.

Add your own:

        Stereotype:
        Resolution:

        Stereotype:
        Resolution:

        Stereotype:
        Resolution:

WORKING WITH MEN

In a survey conducted by the authors, more than 100 women managers were asked what advice they would give to potential women managers about working effectively with men. Here's what they said:

1. *Physical appearance makes a difference.* A crisp, no-nonsense image helps establish positive contact with men. Wear business-like clothing.

2. *Be prepared and organized.* Use strong, direct language and be firm if you are interrupted. Statistics show that women allow themselves to be interrupted 50 percent more often than men. Don't contribute to those statistics.

3. *Use appropriate body language.* Men usually use less body language than women.

4. *Do not respond to flirting.* Keep your conversation and attention directed to the business at hand.

5. *Keep your sense of humor*.* A sense of humor helps keep you ''human''—but don't ''laugh off'' disrespectful or harassing behavior; speak up and voice your objections. If any language or conversation offends, say so.

6. *Avoid discussing feelings.* Personal revelations from business associates is inappropriate.

7. *Don't feel you have to like someone to get the job done.* Concentrate on the job at hand and productivity, not personalities.

8. *Don't be afraid to ask questions or for advice.* No one has all the answers, and honesty is the best approach.

9. *Be prepared to disagree and to stand up for what you believe in.*

**For an excellent book on this topic, order HUMOR AT WORK: Taking Your Job Seriously and Yourself Lightly using the form in the back of this book.*

WORKING WITH MEN (Continued)

SOME MEN ARE EASIER TO WORK
WITH THAN OTHERS—
AND SOME WOMEN ARE,
TOO!

SECTION II

LEADING
YOUR TEAM

> "There are two ways of spreading the light: to be the candle or the mirror that reflects it."
>
> *Edith Wharton*
> Author

THE LEADERSHIP CHALLENGE

Women sometimes avoid seeking leadership because they think that leaders are lonely and exposed to risk.

This image is false. Every leader has followers that provide support and reinforce decisions. The business leader leads her team toward one goal: getting the job done in a timely, positive, ethical, and cost-effective way.

> As a leader, you should inspire the best efforts of your team in order to meet your organization's goals.

RATE YOURSELF AS AN EFFECTIVE TEAM BUILDER

The following attitudes support team building. This scale will help identify your strengths, and determine areas where improvements would be beneficial. Circle the number that best reflects where you fall on the scale. The higher the number, the more the characteristic describes you. When you have finished, total the numbers circled.

1. When I select employees I choose those who can meet the job requirements and work well with others.   7 6 5 4 3 2 1

2. I give employees a sense of ownership by involving them in goal setting, problem solving, and productivity improvement activities.   7 6 5 4 3 2 1

3. I try to provide team spirit by encouraging people to work together and to support one another.   7 6 5 4 3 2 1

4. I talk with people openly and honestly and encourage the same kind of communication in return.   7 6 5 4 3 2 1

5. I keep agreements with my people.   7 6 5 4 3 2 1

6. I help team members get to know each other so they can learn to trust, respect, and appreciate individual talent and ability.   7 6 5 4 3 2 1

7. I insure employees have the required training to do their jobs.   7 6 5 4 3 2 1

8. I understand that conflict within groups is normal, but I work to resolve it quickly and fairly before it can become destructive.   7 6 5 4 3 2 1

9. I believe people will perform as a team when they know what is expected and what benefits they will accrue.   7 6 5 4 3 2 1

10. I am willing to replace members who cannot or will not meet reasonable standards after appropriate coaching.   7 6 5 4 3 2 1

TOTAL: _____

A score between 60 and 70 indicates a positive attitude toward people and the type of attitude needed to build and maintain a strong team. A score between 40 and 59 is acceptable and with reasonable effort, team building should be possible for you. If you scored below 40, you need to carefully examine your attitude.

Adapted from *Team Building: An Exercise in Leadership* by Robert B. Maddux. See the back of this book for ordering information.

CHARACTERISTICS OF HIGHLY-COHESIVE TEAMS

Regardless of the situation or work environment, effective teams demonstrate certain common characteristics. Leaders need to develop these characteristics in their teams. An effective leader makes sure:

☐ Team members understand and share the leader's vision.

☐ Group members respect one another.

☐ Individuals derive satisfaction from being a member of the team.

☐ Communication is open and all members are encouraged to participate in discussions and, where possible, decision-making.

☐ The group has a sense of team pride.

☐ When conflict occurs, it is handled using constructive problem-solving techniques.

☐ Group members are encouraged to cooperate with each other.

☐ Group decision-making and problem-solving is commonly practiced.

☐ The group learns to work together in a relaxed fashion.

☐ Team recognition and credit for a good job is freely given.

☐ Team members understand and share goals, objectives, and mission.

Place a checkmark next to each characteristic your team demonstrates. Are there any characteristics without checkmarks? If so, how do you plan to remedy this?

THE EXPERIENCE OF COLLABORATION

Most people have experiences of collaboration in their lives, even if they don't have it at work. All of us have been involved in collaborative experiences, where everyone was in charge or leadership was shared. Think back to your own work experience as well as outside activities like the PTA, community or church groups, sports, and other activities.

• What were the hallmarks of these activities?

• What got you motivated?

• How did each person in the group get to exercise leadership?

• What are the activities or approaches that increase people's willingness and ability to collaborate?

• What do people do that make you feel less collaborative?

• What are the key elements that make up a collaborative environment?

• How can you cultivate a collaborative environment for team members?

Adapted from *Empowerment: A Practical Guide for Success* by Cynthia D. Scott and Dennis T. Jaffe. See the back of this book for ordering information.

SEVEN BASICS OF TEAM LEADERSHIP

As the leader of your team, you must ensure that the mood of your group is consistently upbeat and the activities it pursues are productive.

Seven ways to help accomplish this are listed below. Check each that you currently do. I make every effort to:

☐ **1.** Treat all employees equally and give each personal attention as required.

☐ **2.** Keep the promises I make to all team members.

☐ **3.** Be consistent and act positively, even if I feel negatively.

☐ **4.** Set a good example and support policies and procedures.

☐ **5.** Stay calm. I understand that others tend to imitate a leader's reactions under pressure.

☐ **6.** Provide opportunities to meet and exchange ideas with my team members.

☐ **7.** Make sure all of my goals are clearly communicated and understood.

If you find yourself not following any of the above basics, take time to decide how to remedy the situation. Leadership, like any other skill, can be continually improved through practice, practice, practice!

CHARACTERISTICS OF TEAM MEMBERS

Each member of any team has individual strengths and weaknesses. As a team leader, you must learn to use your team's attributes to get the job done as efficiently as possible.

You also have your personal characteristics which need to be considered. Use the information you discovered earlier about your style of leadership (page 5) and then apply similar characteristics to your team players. You can best motivate your team to perform when assignments match personalities.

After you read the following descriptions, complete the exercise on page 24. This will help you utilize the diversity of the individual team members.

THE TRADITIONAL TEAM PLAYER:

- prefers a secure situation
- is drawn to close relationships
- changes slowly
- is predictable
- is patient
- likes to identify with the company
- supports the status quo
- is possessive
- looks for loyalty
- likes an easy-going, relaxed atmosphere
- views the team as important

THE ANALYTICAL TEAM PLAYER:

- likes established operating procedures
- does not like sudden change
- believes that precision works
- is accurate at all costs
- has very high standards for self and others
- tends to worry
- is conventional
- tends to hold back opinions unless certain they are right
- is very conscientious
- is a slow decision maker
- takes a rational, problem-solving approach to tasks

CHARACTERISTICS OF TEAM MEMBERS (Continued)

THE DOMINATING TEAM PLAYER:

- likes prestige and position
- is easily bored
- likes challenge and change
- measures worth in terms of accomplishments
- likes direct answers from others
- does not like to be controlled by others
- has high self-assurance
- is very assertive and decisive
- is a good risk-taker
- plays a game to win
- is quick and impatient
- is forceful and demanding

THE CHARISMATIC TEAM PLAYER:

- thrives on popularity and social recognition
- likes freedom from detail and control
- uses intuition well
- is sympathetic
- is friendly
- uses verbal skills well
- is trusting
- is good at persuading and charming people
- acts impulsively and emotionally
- is confident and comfortable with self-promotion
- is enthusiastic

Do you have team members who are being asked to perform duties that seem inappropriate for their personalities?

—How well is this person performing?

—Can you improve this person's performance by altering job duties?

—How else can you help this employee improve?

EVALUATE YOUR TEAM MEMBERS

With the team player characteristics just described, list your team members and their individual styles on the form below:

Name	What is his/her preferred workstyle	How to assign tasks
Example:		
Jim	Dominating	Provide a variety of challenges. Don't oversupervise. Give breathing space.
1.		
2.		
3.		
4.		
5.		
6.		
7.		
8.		

WHAT MOTIVATES YOUR TEAM?

Below are some factors employees mention as motivational. Complete this exercise for yourself and each of your employees. If any additional item motivates you or an employee, add it in the space provided.

Motivator	Motivates Me	Employee A	Employee B	Motivates Employee C	Employee D	Employee E
Financial security	___	___	___	___	___	___
Individual respect	___	___	___	___	___	___
Good work environment	___	___	___	___	___	___
Likes fellow employees	___	___	___	___	___	___
Promotion possibilities	___	___	___	___	___	___
Challenging work	___	___	___	___	___	___
Good benefits	___	___	___	___	___	___
Believes job is important to organization	___	___	___	___	___	___
Management is fair	___	___	___	___	___	___
Job encourages creativity	___	___	___	___	___	___
Recognition	___	___	___	___	___	___
Opportunities for decision making	___	___	___	___	___	___
Good feedback because of regular performance plans and ratings	___	___	___	___	___	___
Job freedom	___	___	___	___	___	___
Opportunity for growth and advancement	___	___	___	___	___	___
Manager is hard-working, honest, and fair	___	___	___	___	___	___
_____	___	___	___	___	___	___

USING VALUES TO MOTIVATE EMPLOYEES

A company's values can motivate employees. However, companies often don't clearly communicate their values to employees. Here's a questionnaire you can use to clarify company values for yourself and employees.

QUESTIONS FOR A GROUP TO CLARIFY VALUES

• What do we stand for?

• What do we mean by ethical behavior?

• What core values are more important than profits?

• What behaviors would mirror these values?

• How do we treat employees? Is this treatment consistent with our values? If not, how can we change?

• How to we treat customers? Is this treatment consistent with our values? If not, how can we change?

• What do we offer employees for their work effort? Is this consistent with our values? If not, how can we change?

• What attitudes and behaviors in employees do we want to reward? Are we? If not, how can we change?

• How do we want to be perceived by the community? Are we so perceived? If not, how can we change?

Adapted from *Organizational Vision, Values and Mission* by Cynthia D. Scott, Dennis T. Jaffe, and Glenn R. Tobe. See the back of this book for ordering information.

SECTION III

PLANNING TOOLS

IF IT ISN'T WRITTEN, IT ISN'T A GOAL

GOALS

Goals are the outcomes you want to achieve. Every successful leader has them. Properly established goals will allow you to move toward your vision. For this to occur, goals must:

- Be clearly stated and attainable.
- Be measurable.
- Be realistic.
- Have deadlines.
- Require action steps.
- Be revised and changed as necessary.
- Be congruent with goals in other areas of your life.

DEFINITION OF A GOAL

"A GOAL is an end toward which you direct some specific EFFORT.
If is a specific and measurable accomplishment to be achieved
within a specific time frame and under specific cost constraints."

ELEMENTS OF A GOAL

- *A goal is a measurable accomplishment to be achieved.*

  What do you expect to be the outcome of your actions? Express this accomplishment with an action verb and include elements that help you measure your success.

  For example: "I reduce operating expense in my department from 2% of sales to 1.5% of sales."

- *Goals include time factors.*

  When do you want to have achieved the goal? Include a specific date by which you will meet your goal.

  For example: "I reduce operating expense in my department from 2% of sales to 1.5% of sales by December 1, 1995."

- *A goal includes cost considerations.*

  How much are you willing to spend to achieve the goal? Cost may be money and/or resources.

  For example, "I reduce operating expense in my department from 2% of sales to 1.5% of sales by December 1, 1995, without reducing staff or without lowering existing levels of customer service."

Adapted from *Goals and Goal Setting: Planning to Succeed* by Larrie A. Rouillard. See the back of this book for ordering information.

GOAL SETTING EXERCISE

Take three goals you have and write them out here, making sure you use these elements: action verbs, measurements, time frames, and cost constraints.

Goal 1: _____

_____

_____

_____

_____

_____

Goal 2: _____

_____

_____

_____

_____

_____

Goal 3: _____

_____

_____

_____

_____

_____

INVOLVE YOUR TEAM IN GOAL SETTING

Goals must reflect personal ownership in order to be meaningful. You cannot effectively and continuously strive toward someone else's goals if you don't have a personal stake in them. That's why you must "own" the goals of your organization if you are to attain them and motivate your team to accept and work toward achieving them.

The roles of team member and leader are outlined below. Circle those concepts with which you agree and are willing to try.

TEAM MEMBER	LEADER
Helps establish performance goals and standards. This is a "self-contract" for achievement as well as a commitment to deliver a result for the team.	Ensures team goals are achievable, but challenging enough to meet organizational needs and provide a sense of accomplishment.
Develops methods to measure results, and checkpoints for control purposes.	Helps balance the complexity of measures and controls with value received.
Outlines the action required to accomplish goals and standards.	Participates with the team to test the action plan's validity against other alternatives.
Specifies participation required from colleagues or in other units within the organization.	Reviews what cooperation and support is required and helps obtain if it required.
Reports progress as work is performed. Seeks guidance and assistance when needed. Adjusts plan as required.	Follows the progress of the work. Reinforces achievement and assists in problem solving when indicated. Ensures targets are met, or modified if circumstances so indicate.

These roles place the responsibility for performance on the appropriate team members. The leader concentrates on leading.

Adapted from *Team Building: An Exercise in Leadership* by Robert B. Maddux. See the back of this book for ordering information.

GETTING ORGANIZED

Stephanie Winston, a well known consultant on managerial productivity and author of *The Organized Executive* says, ''Getting organized is not an end in itself; it is a means to get where you want to be.''

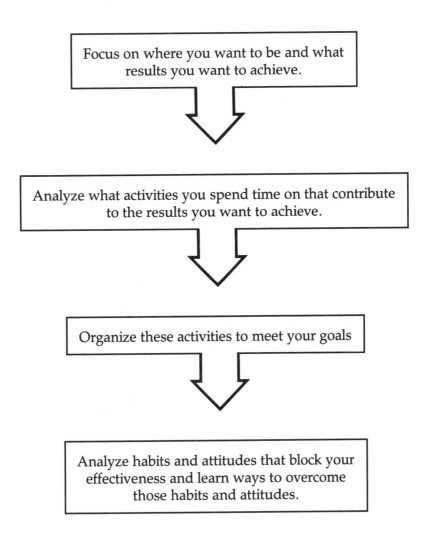

Focus on where you want to be and what results you want to achieve.

Analyze what activities you spend time on that contribute to the results you want to achieve.

Organize these activities to meet your goals

Analyze habits and attitudes that block your effectiveness and learn ways to overcome those habits and attitudes.

LEADERS AND TIME MANAGEMENT

"I must govern the clock, not be governed by it."

Golda Meir
Israeli Prime Minister

LEADERS AND TIME MANAGEMENT

Effective leaders do not travel at reckless speeds...
instead they:

- keep a steady pace,
- expect the unexpected
- know how to delegate for results, and
- don't waste other people's time.

TIME MANAGEMENT (Continued)

Controlling time begins with planning. Every action you perform should take you closer to achieving your goals. These actions should also be prioritized according to the relative importance of your goals. Sometimes, work goals and personal goals conflict with each other for your time. If you have prioritized *all* your goals, you will be better able to deal with such conflicts without feelings of guilt.

You should maintain a calendar or desk journal that allows you to write action steps for your goals each day. You may want to keep a second calendar at home where all family members can log their activities, if appropriate.

Set aside some time each week (i.e. first thing Monday morning), to go over your goals and determine action steps that need to be taken during the coming week. Schedule those steps as if they were appointments to be kept during the week. Also review family or social obligations, if necessary, and decide who will be responsible for coordinating activities for children, friends, etc.

Group common tasks together. For instance, try to set aside a specific time each day to make and return phone calls. This will help eliminate some interruptions.

If you have to be away from your office for a meeting or appointment, identify any errands or other meetings you can schedule in that geographic area. This will eliminate wasted motion and reduce time spent traveling.

---

*For an excellent book on this topic order *Personal Time Management* by Elvin Haynes using the form in the back of this book.

TIME MANAGEMENT (Continued)

WATCH OUT FOR TIME THEFT!

Q. What happens when employees don't know how to do their jobs, can't do their jobs because something prevents them, or don't want to do their jobs?

A. Employees become less productive. They commit "time crime."

Time crime is the disappearance of time at the company's expense. Time crime takes many forms. Do you recognize any of these? Check those you have experienced:

☐ Extra time tacked on to breaks and/or lunch.

☐ Frequent trips to the bathroom.

☐ Lengthy personal phone calls.

☐ Work flow held up by other departments.

☐ Inappropriate staffing for the amount of work; too many or too few employees.

☐ Low morale causing negative attitudes and group complaining sessions.

☐ Procrastination.

If any of these time crimes regularly occur in your unit, write out steps you can take to eliminate time crime from your department.

Adapted from *An Honest Day's Work* by Twyla Dell. See the back of this book for ordering information.

10 COMMANDMENTS OF TIME MANAGEMENT

1. Plan your activities—both work and personal—DAILY.

2. Do high priority actions FIRST.

3. Delegate effectively.

4. Group similar activities—both work and personal—to save time.

5. Handle interruptions efficiently.

6. Say "NO" to non-critical tasks.

7. Eliminate inefficient habits.

8. Mark appointments, meetings, and deadlines on your business calendar and, where appropriate, on your personal calendar and, review them daily.

9. Do ONLY those tasks that are appropriate for your position and responsibility.

10. Balance personal and work responsibilties.

"All my possessions for a moment of time."

Queen Elizabeth I at her death.

LEADERS AND MEETINGS

MEETINGS THAT WORK

A recent study found that managers spend 17 hours a week in meetings, not counting the hours spent preparing for and recovering from meetings.

You don't have much control over other people's meetings, but you can control your own. Effective leaders cultivate the skills of a good meeting leader.

MEET BEFORE A MEETING

Contact associates to garner support for ideas and lay any background you will need to defend your ideas and suggestions. Define who will make formal presentations at the meeting.

PLAN AN AGENDA

Identify the items to be discussed and distribute the agenda to attendees a few days before the meeting. Define how long the meeting should last and the length of time alloted to each speaker, if appropriate.

PREPARE WHAT YOU NEED FOR THE MEETING

If you need charts, numbers, reports, prepare them before you arrive and make sure they are in the room before the meeting starts. Test overhead projectors and other mechanical equipment to make sure it works properly before your attendees arrive.

LEAD THE MEETING

Never lose control of the meeting. Arrive on time and start promptly. If someone tries to monopolize the meeting, suggest that you meet with that person later for a private discussion. If the meeting goes off on a tangent, promptly bring it back on target.

For an excellent book on meetings, order *Effective Meeting Skills* by Marion E. Haynes. See the back of this book for ordering information.

HOW TO DELEGATE SKILLFULLY

DELEGATING

Some managers believe they have to do everything themselves. Women especially are prone to a ''superwoman'' mode of operation. Delegation is the key to getting more done more efficiently.

When you delegate intelligently, you not only exhibit leadership, you also develop the leadership skills of your employees. As a result, your job gets easier and your team becomes more productive.

> WHEN YOU DELEGATE,
> YOUR TEAM MEMBERS LEARN TO TAKE
> RESPONSIBILITY. THE COMMITMENT AND ENERGY
> OF THE TEAM CAN INCREASE DRAMATICALLY.

Effective delegation takes time, patience, and follow-up; but it is worth the effort. Delegation can motivate employees by giving them greater ownership in the organization's productivity.

Delegate tasks when:

- You need more time.
- You want to develop an employee's potential.
- You need to restructure responsibilities to handle a heavy work load.
- You find yourself performing duties more appropriately handed by a direct report.

HOW TO DELEGATE SKILLFULLY
(Continued)

1. Select the project carefully.

Make a list of assignments you feel can be delegated. These may be assignments that take too much of your time or that can be handled effectively by one of your employees. Most assignments should not require constant monitoring or follow-up.

2. Select the person for each task carefully.

Consider all factors involved before selecting the person to whom you will delegate the project.

What is the potential impact on the employee's current workload?
What is the person's current workload?
Will the task be accepted with enthusiasm?
How will co-workers react?
Will the employee have to be relieved of other responsibilities?
How does the task relate to the employee's other duties?

3. Prepare others for the change.

Let employees in your department know that responsibility for each task has been assigned to a co-worker. Explain why the project was delegated.

4. Make the assignment thoughtfully.

Go over the assignment carefully and use examples if possible. Ask if the employee understands the assignment. Ask them to repeat the assignment. Give them the opportunity to ask questions. Convey confidence in the way the employee will handle the new responsibility.

5. Follow up.

Make yourself available to answer questions. Make suggestions when necessary, but allow the employee freedom to manage the assignment. Coach the employee if the task is not being performed satisfactorily. Refer others to the employee if they have questions about the task. Compliment the employee when the task has been satisfactorily completed. Make sure the employee is given credit for his/her success at performance review time.

You can delegate authority, but you cannot delegate responsibility. As long as you are responsible, you must know how things are going.

HOW TO DELEGATE SKILLFULLY
(Continued)

RATE YOURSELF AS A DELEGATOR

Answer:
- A. Most of the time
- B. Sometimes
- C. Rarely/Never

_____ 1. Do you take work home?

_____ 2. Do you work significantly longer hours than your staff?

_____ 3. Do you do the work of others because you can do it faster or better?

_____ 4. When you return to work from an absence is your in-basket overflowing?

_____ 5. Do you continue to handle activities you had from previous jobs?

_____ 6. Do employees constantly interrupt you with questions about their projects or assignments?

_____ 7. Do you perform routine tasks others could easily handle?

_____ 8. Are you slow in meeting deadlines?

_____ 9. Do you feel the need to keep an eye on every activity in your unit?

_____ 10. Are you poor at setting priorities?

_____ 11. Are you uncomfortable when your employees don't have enough to do?

_____ 12. Do you hear criticism about your lack of delegation?

Note any items you answered with A's and list areas you identify for improvement: i.e. I will do a better job of delegating tasks and training employees in order to eliminate interruptions.

1.

2.

3.

DECISION MAKING AND LEADERSHIP

Most decisions involve an element of risk or uncertainty*. No matter how much information you have, you cannot absolutely guarantee the outcome. Good leaders are good decision makers even when it means taking a risk. The following steps will help you develop your decision making skills. To become a more effective leader, I will:

☐ Identify available options before making a decision.

☐ Seek alternative options from team players.

☐ Encourage discussion over alternative options to stimulate creativity.

☐ Test each option against the situation.

☐ Identify who will assume responsibility for taking action based on a decision.

☐ Build in feedback mechanisms to assess the effectiveness of the decision.

☐ Make a decision.

---

*For an excellent book on this subject, order *Systematic Problem-Solving and Decision-Making* by Sandy Pokras using the order form in the back of this book.

SECTION IV

LEADERS ARE PROBLEM SOLVERS

> "Opportunities are usually disguised as hard work, so most people don't recognize them."
>
> *Ann Landers*
> Columnist

EIGHT STEPS TO EFFECTIVE PROBLEM SOLVING

1. Accept the problem as an opportunity to improve a situation.

2. Solicit the perceptions of those affected and identify differences.

3. Define the problem as specifically as possible.

4. Analyze why the problem exists, obtain facts, and identify barriers to resolution.

5. Brainstorm possible solutions.

6. Set criteria for the ultimate solution.

7. Select the solution that best meets the criteria.

8. Make the decision and install a means to measure the outcome.

CONFLICT RESOLUTION STYLES

There are five basic approaches to conflict resolution. They are summarized below. Indicate the one you are most likely to use with employees with an E, your peers with a P, with your manager, an S, and with family members with an F.

STYLE	CHARACTERISTIC BEHAVIOR	USER JUSTIFICATION	E,P,S, or F?
Avoidance	Non-confrontational. Ignores or passes over issues. Denies issues are a problem.	Differences too minor or too great to resolve. Attempts might damage relationships or create even greater problems.	
Accommodating	Agreeable, non-assertive behavior. Cooperative even at the expense of personal goals.	Not worth risking damage to relationships or general disharmony.	
Win/Lose	Confrontational, assertive and aggressive. Must win at any cost.	Survival of the fittest. Must prove superiority. Most ethically or professionally correct.	
Compromising	Important all parties achieve basic goals and maintain good relationships. Aggressive but cooperative.	No one person or idea is perfect. There is more than one good way to do anything. You must give to get.	
Problem Solving	Needs of both parties are legitimate and important. High respect for mutual support. Assertive and cooperative.	When parties will openly discuss issues, a mutually beneficial solution can be found without anyone making a major concession.	

From *Team Building: An Exercise in Leadership* by Robert B. Maddux. See the back of this book for ordering information.

CONFLICT EXERCISE

1. With whom do you have or have had a conflict? Use examples from both business and personal life.

a. _____

b. _____

c. _____

2. What is or was the essence of the conflict?

a. _____

b. _____

c. _____

Choose one of your conflicts identified above and complete the following.
Describe the conflict resolution style which would have been most effective in the conflict you identified. Did you use it?

1. _____

2. _____

3. _____

RESOLVING CONFLICT

Each of us operates from a unique perspective. Even if everyone has agreed on a goal or decision, disagreements can arise. When this happens it is essential to know how to resolve a conflict if you plan to be an effective leader. One stereotype you often hear about female employees is that they look for ways to avoid conflict. Strong leaders, male or female, need to be proficient at conflict resolution. Don't allow yourself to follow the stereotype.

Here are seven steps to help you resolve conflicts:

- Schedule a meeting with the other party to discuss the situation.

- When you meet, initiate a discussion that acknowledges there is a conflict.

- Use ''I'' statements to avoid accusations. Encourage the other party to use ''I'' statements, too.

- Ask direct questions that require the other party to talk about the situation.

- Repeat what you are hearing. ''Based on what you've told me, this is how you see the situation.'' This is a good way to confirm that you understand what you are hearing.

- Tell the other party what you want as an outcome and ask what they want.

- Agree to work toward a resolution and schedule a meeting, if required, to follow-up on the situation.

MANAGING DIFFICULT PEOPLE

Difficult people are everywhere. They can be negative, irritating, seemingly impossible to manage, and create stress for everyone around them.

Sometimes it seems easier to avoid or ''work around'' difficult people, but this is never a good long-term solution. If you learn to assess the person's behavior and listen with genuine interest, it is possible to effectively manage every difficult person. Good leaders never avoid difficult management situations.

To help you learn how to manage difficult people, following are seven difficult personality types. In all seven cases, the behavior of each type is described first, followed by effective action you can take to handle each type of behavior.

SEVEN DIFFICULT PERSONALITY TYPES

1. ATTACKERS

Behavior: Attackers assert their viewpoint forcefully. They require people to listen to what they say. They need room and time to blow off steam.

Your Action: Address the attacker by name and quietly, but firmly, ask him or her to sit. Then listen carefully to what the attacker has to say. Once calmed, the attacker usually becomes reasonable and may suggest valuable solutions. The worst coping behavior on your part would be to return the attack.

2. EGOTISTS

Behavior: Egotists also assert themselves, but unlike attackers, they may be subject experts.

Your Action: Show honest respect for their knowledge, but don't become intimidated by it. Instead, capitalize on what they know by asking questions. Compliment them when they provide helpful information but make sure they know you are the leader.

SEVEN DIFFICULT PERSONALITY TYPES (Continued)

3. SNEAKS

Behavior: Sneaks take "potshots" and often use sarcasm as a weapon.

Your Action: Confront sneaks with direct questions and let them know you do not appreciate their sarcasm. Use positive reinforcement when possible to steer them toward becoming more of a team player.

4. VICTIMS

Behavior: Victims see everything negatively. They act powerless and defeated, often whining about everyone and everything.

Your Action: Ask them for suggestions to improve the situation. Have them state the negatives and address each logically and positively.

5. NEGATORS

Behavior: Negators are usually suspicious of those in authority and believe that their way of doing things is the only way.

Your Action: Let negators use their negative "ammunition" in a group meeting, then let co-workers express their views about possible solutions. They will usually try to "enlighten" negators that better solutions exist.

6. SUPER-AGREEABLE PEOPLE

Behavior: Super-agreeable people have such a strong need to be liked that they do whatever you request at the expense of their own needs. They will overcommit and often disappoint and frustrate everyone.

Your Action: Monitor assignments to make sure they are not overworked.

7. UNRESPONSIVE PEOPLE

Behavior: Unresponsive people are the most difficult people to manage. They are seemingly impossible to draw out.

Your Action: Use open-ended questions that require more than a "Yes" or "No" answer. Wait for a response. Resist the urge to finish sentences for them. Follow-up on actions assigned to them and give them assignments to present at future meetings.

DIFFICULT PEOPLE LEADERSHIP EXERCISE

List some difficult people you must work with and identify their dominate, difficult trait.

Person	Trait
1.	1.
2.	2.
3.	3.
4.	4.
5.	5.

Then review the strategies for each type of difficult person and summarize how you can more effectively approach each of these people in the future.

1.

2.

3.

4.

5.

COACHING AND COUNSELING

Effective leaders know how to coach and how to counsel employees*. Even more important, they understand the differences between these skills and when to use each. Following are brief definitions of coaching and counseling.

> **Counseling:** A supportive process by a manager to help an employee define and work through personal problems that affect job performance.

> **Coaching:** A directive process by a manager to train and orient an employee to the realities of the workplace and to help the employee remove barriers to optimum work performance.

Counseling and coaching share many of the same skills. At times they may seem to overlap. When they do, remember the following diagrams. They will help you differentiate these two processes.

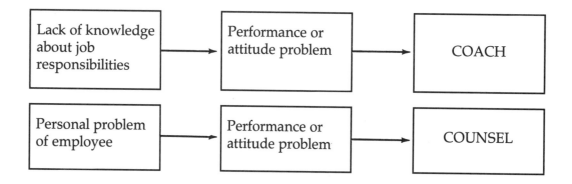

---

*Information of Coaching and Counseling skills was adapted from Marianne Minor's book *Coaching and Counseling*. To order this book, use the form at the back of this book.

COACHING AND COUNSELING
(Continued)

THE BENEFITS OF COACHING

Why should you improve your coaching skills if you are a leader? See if you agree with the authors by deciding which statements are true and which are false. Compare your answers with those of the authors at the bottom of the page.

COACHING...

True *False*

☐ ☐ 1. Makes your job easier when employees build their skill levels.

☐ ☐ 2. Enables greater delegation so you can have more time to truly manage versus ''do for.''

☐ ☐ 3. Builds your reputation as a ''people developer.''

☐ ☐ 4. Increases productivity when employees know what the goals are and how to achieve them.

☐ ☐ 5. Develops sharing of leadership responsibilities.

☐ ☐ 6. Positive recognition and feedback increases employee motivation and initiative.

☐ ☐ 7. Increases likelihood of tasks being completed in a quality way.

☐ ☐ 8. Avoids surprises and defensiveness in performance appraisals.

☐ ☐ 9. Increases creativity and innovation of unit as employees feel safe to take risks.

☐ ☐ 10. Increases team cohesiveness due to clarified goals and roles.

Answers: All ten statements are true.

PROMOTING DIVERSITY TO IMPROVE MORALE AND PRODUCTIVITY

People want to feel that they are important and that their contribution matters. Recognizing and using people's abilities and experiences involves them in a way that builds rapport, respect, ownership, and loyalty. The higher morale is, the harder employees are likely to work. Better productivity results.

Businesses receive many benefits by recognizing and encouraging work force diversity. Among the many benefits, consider the economic impact of these top three:

- Tapping into tremendous purchasing power.
  - Older Americans spend more than $800 billion annually.
  - Minority markets buy more goods and services than any country that trades with the U.S.
  - Understanding different values and perspectives opens new markets.

- Reducing costs by reducing employee turnover.
  - Highly trained workers will stay with organizations that are responsive to their needs.
  - Retaining is expensive.
  - High employee turnover reduces morale and productivity.

- Receiving the benefits of productivity, creativity, and innovation from all employees.
  - New perspectives enhance problem solving.
  - Business success is often dependent on group performance.
  - An inclusive environment builds respect, ownership, and loyalty.

Adapted from *Dynamics of Diversity: Strategic Programs for Your Organization* by Odette Pollar and Rafael Gonzalez. See the back of this book for ordering information.

THE ART OF FEEDBACK AND USING ''I'' MESSAGES

Leaders understand how important feedback is. They also know, to be effective, feedback must be specific. It should also convey your true feelings. When delivering critical messages, it is especially important to let your employee know exactly how you feel about the situation—otherwise you are not being honest. For example, if one of your staff is continually late, you could pass the buck by saying—''My boss has noticed you are not always on time for work and asked me to let you know this is against company regulations.'' This would be transparent management, where you simply allowed a message from a higher authority to ''pass through'' you to your employee. A more effective approach would be an ''I'' message similar to the following:

> ''When you are late to work, I feel frustrated because others must pick up the slack for you. Is there some reason you can't be on time?''

''I'' messages are helpful because the person you are addressing feels less defensive. ''I feel...(annoyed, angry, hurt, upset)'' or ''In my opinion, I believe, I think...'' give more direct feedback.

Rewrite the following statements using ''I'' messages instead of ''you'' messages.

Example: ''You never pay attention to my instructions''

> ''Based on your last report, I feel you are not paying enough attention to my instructions. Do you agree?''

1. You always make me mad.

_____

2. You really hurt my feelings.

_____

3. You are too bossy.

_____

"I" MESSAGES (Continued)

TALKING ABOUT HOW YOU FEEL

Women often stiffle their feelings because they are afraid of being branded as too emotional. Being emotional is acceptable, as long as it is expressed appropriately. That's what "I" messages allow you to do.

You must identify what you are feeling as specifically as possible. Ask yourself, "What am I feeling—mad, sad, glad, or scared?" This question will help you describe your feelings quickly and accurately.

The following vocabulary of emotions will help you better identify and express your feelings in a direct, open, and honest manner.

MAD	SAD	GLAD	SCARED	COMBINATION
irritated	depressed	pleased	anxious	guilty
annoyed	unhappy	happy	worried	jealous
angry	disappointed	joyful	fearful	frustrated
ticked off	hurt	delighted	afraid	embarrassed
miffed	down	up	nervous	uncomfortable
upset	stressed	excited	uncertain	confused

ADD YOUR OWN:

MAD	SAD	GLAD	SCARED	COMBINATION

HOW TO USE POSITIVE ANGER

Leaders sometimes feel frustration or disappointment and respond with anger. Effectively expressing anger is difficult for many women who were reared to "turn the other cheek" or "be nice." Often women don't believe that anger is a natural, honest feeling and don't realize that it can be an important safety valve. Some women may avoid expressing anger for fear of appearing emotional or of crying.

Expressing anger can work for you or against you, depending on how you express it and with whom.

You can use anger to gain attention and make a point if you normally handle situations cooly and professionally and if you are acting from conviction for something significant that benefits your organization—for instance, fighting for a project you deeply believe in.

Following are some techniques for expressing anger productively and effectively.

- Admit your angry feelings to yourself.

- Take deep breaths to calm yourself.

- If you begin to lose control, "drop" your pen (or some similar momentary action) and as you bend over to get it, regain your composure.

- Take a break and do something physically vigorous or highly creative. When you engage in physical or mental exercise, you help dissipate your anger.

- Prepare to confront the person or situation that caused you to feel angry. Once things get "aired", things usually improve.

Tantrums and outbursts should be few and far between, or people will classify you as a difficult person. But if you lose control and "blow up," then after you cool off, apologize—not for how you feel, but for your outburst.

> "The filaments of anger affect the entire web of our social relations."
>
> *Carol Tavris*
> Author

"STRESSBUSTERS"

Leaders often feel stress. Women leaders are particularly vulnerable because they often carry heavy workloads both on the job *and* at home.

Before you can act effectively at home or on the job, you must be able to control stress.

Use the following "stressbusters" whenever you feel your stress level rising.

- **Be present.** You can only live in the moment. Worrying about the past or future is not productive. When you concentrate on the present, you don't allow time for stressful fretting.

- **Grow, or let go.** When you are criticized, don't take it personally. Analyze it. Does the criticism repeat criticism you have heard previously? If so, perhaps it is valid and points out an area that needs work. If not, and if you believe the criticism is unjust, let it go. You can't change some people's minds if they choose to be unfair.

- **Do your personal best** and don't compare your performance with others. Trust yourself and your abilities.

- **Don't let tensions build up** inside until you feel like bursting. Get another person's opinion to help you put the situation in perspective.

- **Your life isn't the job.** At least it shouldn't be. When your work life takes a turn for the worst, rely on your home life and personal relationships to bolster you. And vice versa.

- **Expand your world.** Exercise, take up a hobby, go to a movie, plan regular evenings out with a friend or loved one.

TIPS TO OVERCOME STRESS

At work:	At home:
Take short breaks	Develop leisure interests
Add variety to your duties	Maintain personal relationships
Develop a support system	Leave your work at the office
Keep yourself detached	Keep physically fit
Develop positive work habits	Talk and play with loved ones
Encourage positive feedback	Encourage open communication

SECTION V

DEVELOPING PERSONAL POWER

> "Success is important only to the extent that it puts one in a position to do more things one likes to do."
>
> *Sarah Caldwell*
> Conductor

BALANCING HOME AND CAREER

One of your most difficult challenges is to balance your career and your personal life. You want to establish a smooth flow between the two to be truly successful. This requires you to develop personal power.

Balancing a family and career can challenge the best leader. Avoid falling into the Superwoman trap by learning to treat domestic arrangements as management challenges, not personal crises.

- Hire household help if you need it.
- Accept the fact that many little things just won't get done.
- Learn to be imperfect. It can be most freeing.
- Develop a sense of humor.

For an excellent book on balancing personal and work life, order *Balancing Home and Career* by Pam Conrad. See the back of this book for ordering information.

DEVELOPING PERSONAL POWER

Developing a sense of personal power involves developing a belief in yourself. You should believe that you can go after what you want and that you have the ability to reach your goals in your own way.

A powerful woman leader empowers others and provides a safe environment for them to express their opinions. The personally powerful leader encourages her staff to set goals, express themselves openly, and be important contributors to the work unit. Her employees feel supported and acknowledged.

You develop a sense of personal power by developing authority, accessability, assertiveness, a positive image, and solid communication habits. We will look at each of these traits briefly in the following pages.

1. AUTHORITY
Authority is inner confidence—a trust in your skills and abilities.

Authority begins inside, with an attitude of ''I can do it; I deserve success.'' This attitude radiates outwardly as you assert your rights, as you ask for what you need and want, and as you develop a willingness to give to others and yourself.

Many women tend to discount their successes and are often embarrassed by proclaiming their talents and strengths.

The image of Rocky bouncing around the ring, arms upraised in victory, is a male image. But women must stop denigrating their skills and talents; they must feel comfortable with the power they have earned.

PERSONAL POWER (Continued)

2. ASSERTIVENESS: A KEY SKILL

It would be nice if you could simply decide to go down the road marked "Assertive" and live your life without straying from the path. Women leaders must learn to hold their own in a positive way by learning assertiveness.

Real life is full of twists and turns and *no one is consistently assertive.* All of us use the three basic behavior styles described below depending on the situation and personal factors. The good news is that *we can learn to become more assertive more of the time.*

1. NONASSERTIVE behavior is passive and indirect. It communicates a message of inferiority. By being nonassertive we allow the wants, needs, and rights of others to be more important than our own. Nonassertive behavior helps create "win-lose" situations. A person behaving nonassertively will lose or at best be disregarded while allowing the other to win. Following this road leads to being a victim, not a winner.

2. AGGRESSIVE behavior is more complex. It can be either active or passive. Aggression can be direct or indirect, honest or dishonest—but it always communicates an impression of superiority and disrespect. By being aggressive we put our wants, needs, and rights above those of others. We attempt to get our way by not allowing others a choice. Aggressive behavior is usually inappropriate because it violates the rights of others. People behaving aggressively may "win" by making sure others "lose"—but in doing so, set themselves up for retaliation. No one likes a bully.

3. ASSERTIVE behavior is active, direct, and honest. It communicates an impression of self-respect and respect for others. By being assertive we view our wants, needs, and rights as equal with those of others. We work toward "win-win" outcomes. An assertive person wins by influencing, listening, and negotiating so that others choose to cooperate willingly. This behavior leads to success without retaliation and encourages honest, open relationships!

Here are some guidelines you can follow to increase your assertiveness leadership skills.

- Make time for yourself. Assert your right to take care of your own needs. This helps you develop a healthy self-respect.
- Ask for help when you need it. Become a team player and let others know you do not work in a vacuum.
- Say "No" without feeling guilty.
- Express your feelings openly. This involves risktaking and demonstrates a high level of integrity.
- Request feedback as a way to grow and learn. This will develop an openness to change.
- Ask for what you need and want. Focus on your goals, developing a sense of purpose and commitment.
- Look for win-win situations.

*Adapted from *Developing Positive Assertiveness* by Sam R. Lloyd. See the back of this book for ordering information.

PERSONAL POWER (Continued)

3. ACCESSIBILITY

You have probably heard the adage about "being in the right place at the right time." It is true, and effective leaders know how to make it happen. People do business with people they know, and the powerful woman leader is a master networker. By learning to develop skills as a team player, it is possible to increase visibility. Good networkers also give themselves a valuable circle of people from whom to seek information and support.

You probably have more contacts than you realize. Imagine yourself as the hub of a wheel, surrounded by spokes of contacts. List every key person you know and every organization you belong to in a graphic similar to the one shown below. Make sure your list takes into account anyone or any organization that can help you reach your goals. Establish a goal to contact at least three people on your list each week to maintain your network.

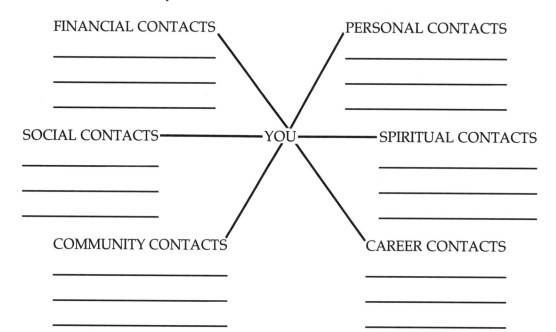

Accessibility also means letting your world—your organization, religious unit, industry or professional group or community know who you are. Volunteer, write articles, join committees. To become successful, you must network, network, network!

- Join your industry association.
- Subscribe to trade publications.
- Join business organizations such as the Chamber of Commerce.
- Write articles for magazines and newspapers.
- Add your own _____

PERSONAL POWER (Continued)

4. IMAGE

You communicate inner authority to others through your image. Effective leaders communicate their authority. Are you projecting the image consistent with a strong leader? Is your voice firm or little girl cute? Worse, do you whine?

Is your speech littered with slang or do you hesitate with vocal "uhhhhhhs?"

If your job requires phone contact, replay each voice mail message you leave to monitor your speech patterns and tone of voice.

When you meet with people, make direct eye contact when you speak with them. Keep your handshake firm and friendly.

You can never fully erase a first impression, so it is very important to project the best possible image the first time around.

> "Remember, Ginger Rogers did everything Fred Astaire did, but she did it backwards and in high heels."
>
> *Faith Whittlesey*
> Politician

PERSONAL POWER (Continued)

5. SOLID COMMUNICATION HABITS

Pay attention to how you speak and how you act as you speak. Often non-verbal signals say more than words do. Make sure your body isn't saying something different from your mouth.

Practice the following good communication habits until they become second nature:

- Look people in the eye.
- Keep your facial expression consistent with your message.
- Stand erect and move energetically.
- Speak with an even pace and enunciate clearly.
- Use only body movements and gestures necessary to make your point, but no more.

Practice projecting authority. You will not be accepted as a leader until you learn to communicate clearly and directly—in writing, in speaking, in listening and through the professional image you present. It is all a form of communication.

> "I like people who refuse to speak until they are ready to speak."
>
> *Lillian Hellman*
> Playwright

SECTION VI

SUMMARY—
HAVING IT ALL

A LEADER

- keeps her objectives clear and attainable.
- balances and limits tasks to avoid harmful stress.
- assigns priorities for maximum payoffs.
- evaluates her behavior to ensure it is appropriate.
- revises and changes her plans as necessary.
- visualizes achievement of her goals.
- knows the difference between failure and learning.
- has convictions and acts on them.
- has fun.

THE BENEFITS OF BEING A WOMAN LEADER

As you cultivate personal power, professional and positional power follow. You create "win-win" situations for yourself and those around you. By embracing and expressing your power to the world, you become the powerful person you want to be.

Your life is more interesting and satisfying because you will have opportunities to grow. You will experience things such as travel, interesting classes, and seminars. Your horizons will expand in all directions.

You will meet more diverse and interesting people. With greater responsibility and visibility, you will be more in demand. Virtually every organization is looking for women with strong leadership abilities.

You will also look better! When a woman feels successful with her accomplishments, she adds a confident aura that makes her more attractive.

You will enjoy a greater income and the increased freedom that goes with it.

> Your self-esteem will be enhanced.
> Your career opportunities will multiply.
> You become more comfortable with power.

All of these are reasons for you to become the best woman leader possible. It's up to you. Good luck!

"I still want to do my work. I still want to do my livingness. And I have lived. I have been fulfilled. I recognized what I had, and I never sold it short."

Louise Nevelson
Artist

PROFESSIONAL DEVELOPMENT —SUMMARY REVIEW

Answer these final questions as honestly as possible. They will help guide you to apply what you have learned from this book. Briefly write your responses in the space provided.

1. What are your personal career objectives?

2. What new skills have you learned recently which will help you achieve your goals?

3. What training have you taken to enhance your professionalism?

4. What training do you plan to take this year?

5. What professional literature have you read in the past few months?

6. What networks or organizations do you now belong to?

7. What are your plans for professional development in the next year?

8. How do you intend to apply what you have learned from this book to your leadership skills?

YOUR FEEDBACK IS IMPORTANT

This book is the result of feedback from hundreds of people in trainings and seminars. Feedback is vital to be of continuing value. For this reason, please take a moment and note three pluses and one to three suggestions to improve the next revision of this book.

+ _____

+ _____

+ _____

Suggestions:

1. _____

2. _____

3. _____

Thank you for your input.

Please mail to: Marilyn Manning, Ph. D.
Leadership Skills for Women
c/o CRISP PUBLICATIONS, INC.
1200 Hamilton Court
Menlo Park, California 94025

READING LIST

The authors recommend the following materials.

Arapakis, Maria. *Softpower! How to Speak Up, Set Limits, and Say No Without Losing Your Lover, Your Job, or Your Friend.* Warner Books. 1990.

Bramson, Robert M. *Coping with Difficult People.* Anchor Books. New York. 1981.

Briles, Judith. *The Confidence Factor: How Self Esteem Can Change Your Life.* MasterMedia Limited. New York. 1990.

Dreher, Diane. *The Tao of Inner Peace.* HarperPerennial. New York. 1990.

Fisher, Roger & Ury, William. *Getting to Yes.* Houghton. Boston. 1981.

Friedman, M.D., Meyer and Ulmer, Diane. *Treating Type A Behavior and Your Heart.* Ballatine. NY. 1984.

Galginaitis, Carol R. *Managing the Demands of Work and Home.* Irwin Professional Publishing. Burr Ridge, IL. 1994.

Gilligan, Carol. *In a Different Voice.* Harvard University Press. Cambridge, MA. 1982.

Haddock, Patricia, and Johns, Connie, editors. *Managing Employees: A Step-by-Step Guide to Personnel Procedures for the Small Business in California.* Easy Street Publishing. San Francisco. 1994.

Jampolsky, Gerald, M.D. *Love is Letting Go of Fear.* Bantam. New York. 1979.

Jeffers, Susan. *Feel the Fear and Do It Anyway.* Fawcett Columbine. New York. 1987.

Manning, Marilyn. *Personal Power Strategies.* (cassettes) Marilyn Manning. Mountain View, CA. 1991.

Manning, Marilyn. *Using Stress and Conflict Positively.* (cassettes) Marilyn Manning. Mountain View, CA. 1992.

Manning, Marilyn, and Haddock, Patricia. *Office Management.* Crisp Publications. Menlo Park, CA. 1990.

Marone, Nicky. *Women and Risk.* St. Martin's Press. New York. 1992.

READING LIST (Continued)

Popcorn, Faith. *The Popcorn Report.* Harper Collins. 1991.

Radin, Bill. *Breakaway Careers.* Career Press. New Jersey. 1994.

RoAne, Susan. *The Secrets of Savvy Networking.* Warner. 1993.

Roddick, Anita. *Body and Soul.* Crown Publishers, Inc. New York. 1991.

Sher, Barbara. *Wishcraft.* Ballantine Books. New York. 1979.

Silver, A. David. *Enterprising Women: Lessons from 100 of the Greatest Entrepreneurs of our Day.* AMACOM. 1994.

Timm, Paul. *50 Ways to Win New Customers.* Career Press. New Jersey. 1993.

Waterman, Jr., Robert H. *The Renewal Factor: How the Best Get and Keep the Competitive Edge.* Bantam Books. NY. 1987.

Wheatley, Margaret J. *Leadership and the New Science.* Berret-Koehler Publishers Inc. San Francisco. 1994.

Weider, Marcia. *Making Your Dreams Come True.* Mastermedia Limited. New York. 1993.

Wilson, Susan. *Goal Setting.* AMACOM. 1994.

Ziglar, Zig. *Top Performance.* Berkley Books. New York. 1986.

For information on any of the above books or tapes, write to Marilyn Manning, 945 Mountain View Avenue, Mountain View, CA 94040. Phone: (415) 965-3663.

NOTES

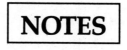

NOTES

NOTES

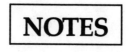

NOTES

NOW AVAILABLE FROM
CRISP PUBLICATIONS

Books • Videos • CD Roms • Computer-Based Training Products

If you enjoyed this book, we have great news for you. There are over 200 books available in the *50-Minute*™ Series. To request a free full-line catalog, contact your local distributor or Crisp Publications, Inc., 1200 Hamilton Court, Menlo Park, CA 94025. Our toll-free number is 800-422-7477.

Subject Areas Include:

Management

Human Resources

Communication Skills

Personal Development

Marketing/Sales

Organizational Development

Customer Service/Quality

Computer Skills

Small Business and Entrepreneurship

Adult Literacy and Learning

Life Planning and Retirement

CRISP WORLDWIDE DISTRIBUTION

English language books are distributed worldwide. Major international distributors include:

ASIA/PACIFIC

Australia/New Zealand: In Learning, PO Box 1051 Springwood QLD, Brisbane, Australia 4127
Telephone: 7-841-1061, Facsimile: 7-841-1580
ATTN: Mssrs. Gordon

Singapore: Graham Brash (Pvt) Ltd. 32, Gul Drive, Singapore 2262
Telphone: 65-861-1336, Facsimile: 65-861-4815
ATTN: Mr. Campbell

EUROPEAN UNION

England: Flex Training, Ltd. 9-15 Hitchin Street, Baldock, Hertfordshire, SG7 6AL
Telephone: 1-462-896000, Facsimile: 1-462-892417
ATTN: Mr. Willets

INDIA

Multi-Media HRD, Pvt., Ltd., National House, Tulloch Road, Appolo Bunder, Bombay, India 400-039
Telephone: 91-22-204-2281, Facsimile: 91-22-283-6478
ATTN: Mssrs. Aggarwal

MIDDLE EAST

United Arab Emirates: Al-Mutanabbi Bookshop, PO Box 71946, Abu Dhabi
Telephone: 971-2-321-519, Facsimile: 971-2-317-706

NORTH AMERICA

Canada: Reid Publishing, Ltd., Box 69559-109 Thomas Street, Oakville, Ontario Canada L6J 7R4.
Telephone: (905) 842-4428, Facsimile: (905) 842-9327

SOUTH AMERICA

Mexico: Grupo Editorial Iberoamerica, Serapio Rendon #125, Col. San Rafael, 06470 Mexico, D.F.
Telephone: 525-705-0585, Facsimile: 525-535-2009
ATTN: Señor Grepe

SOUTH AFRICA

Alternative Books, Unit A3 Sanlam Micro Industrial Park, Hammer Avenue STRYDOM Park, Randburg, 2194 South Africa
Telephone: 2711 792 7730, Facsimile: 2711 792 7787
ATTN: Mr. de Haas

Selected Crisp titles are available in 23 languages. For more information contact International Publishing Manager, Suzanne Kelly-Lyall at (415) 323-6100.